Sweet Temptation

Sweet Temptation

25 recipes for homemade sweets, chocolates and other delicious treats

ICKI TRENCH

CICO BOOKS
LONDON NEW YORK

Kitchen safety

If you're experienced in the kitchen, you're probably used to tasting as you cook. However, sugar reaches a far higher temperature than everyday cooking. Sugar hardens as soon as it cools, so if you dip your finger in liquid sugar, it will not only burn, but stick to you. An automatic reaction is to lick off the sugar – resulting in another burn to your lips. Be aware of the extremely high temperatures involved and supervise children at all times.

Published in 2009 by CICO Books
an imprint of Ryland Peters & Small
20–21 Jockey's Fields
London WC1R 4BW

www.cicobooks.co.uk

10 9 8 7 6 5 4 3 2 1

A CIP catalogue record for this book is available from the British Library

ISBN-13: 978 1 906525 49 1

Printed in China

Project Editor: Gillian Haslam
Text Editor: Katie Hardwicke
Designer: Roger Hammond,
bluegumdesigners.com
Photographer: Winfried Heinze
Stylists: Sue Rowlands and
Rose Hammick

Dedicated to my sweet, loving, delicious daughters, Camilla and Maddy

Author's Acknowledgements

So many thanks to so many people who helped in making this book. It was a fun and easy task to devise the recipes, then a little daunting to get them all looking perfect for photography. Several projects were left around the house, so my big thanks to my family and any passing guests for offering to eat them all up.

To Caroline Cowan, who saved the day, assisting me in trying out the recipes and helping to make the sweets look fantastic. Also huge thanks to Rebecca Hawes and Matthew Barr, who meticulously and expertly made some fantastic candy and chocolates; and thanks to Klaryssa Vidler who is now a master of the art of making chocolate Easter eggs.

To Winfried Heinze for his amazing photography that has made this book and sweets look as wonderful as they taste and to Rose Hammick, who expertly styled them. Finally, to Cindy Richards for having the confidence to commission me to write this book and to Gillian Haslam for making it all happen with such charming ease.

Contents

Introduction

Who can resist the enticing smell of caramelized sugar or melted chocolate lingering in the kitchen air, or the squeals of delight from children when they see the evolving shape of a sugar mouse or an Easter egg? The art of home-made sweet making is back.

Certainly, sweets of all shapes, sizes and descriptions are easy to buy in large stores and supermarkets, where the displays groan with confectionery loaded with bright artificial colours and flavourings. There are plenty of companies that offer naturally-flavoured and coloured confectionary, too. However, there's nothing quite like making, eating or giving your own home-made sweets – they will look and taste even better than the shop-bought staples. Whether you serve them as an everyday treat or a seasonal gift, they're bound to be a success.

You don't have to be a sugar specialist to follow the recipes in this book. The joy of sweet making is that the sweets don't have to be the perfect shape or size to look and taste delicious. You can get started with a few pieces of equipment that you will probably have in your cupboards already: a heavy-based saucepan, a wooden spoon, kitchen scales and a measuring jug are all you'll need. In addition, the one piece of specialist equipment that I would definitely recommend buying is a good-quality metal sugar thermometer (see page 64) – avoid glass thermometers as they easily break.

Most of the recipes follow standard cooking techniques, however cooking sugar and melting chocolate need a little extra expertise. The temperature of cooked sugar is crucial – have patience and watch the thermometer closely (see page 64).

Chocolate-making is an art and there are all sorts of specialist methods. In the recipes in this book, I have kept the use of chocolate very simple, using melted chocolate as a coating or forming the basis of the sweet once cooled. A bain-marie isn't essential as you can easily make your own by melting the chocolate in a bowl placed above a saucepan of gently simmering water. Do use a good-quality plain chocolate if possible, with at least 65 per cent cocoa solids.

Whichever recipe you decide to try, I guarantee you will be seduced by the lure of cooking sweets and chocolates and will marvel at how the recipes evolve into a magic world that rolls around your tongue and melts in your mouth.

Sugar roses

Sugar roses make pretty gifts on their own, or you can use them to decorate cup cakes, wedding or birthday cakes or give them as wedding favours. You can either make your own fondant icing or buy it ready-made from most grocery shops.

INGREDIENTS

MAKES 8 ROSES

125 g (4¹/₂ oz) fondant icing

Food colouring in several colours (optional)

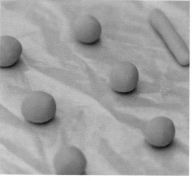

1 Divide the icing into four equal pieces and add a different food colouring to each, if required. Take one coloured piece and knead the icing so that it is smooth without any cracks. Roll the icing into a sausage shape, approximately 23 cm (9 in) long. Cut it in half, cut into quarters, then cut each quarter in half, and then cut each eighth in half – you should be left with 16 pieces.

2 Roll eight pieces into balls and one piece into a small sausage shape approximately 5 cm (2 in) long. The excess icing can be added to the remaining icing and re-rolled to make another rose. Place the eight balls on the top half of a cellophane bag in two rows of four, with the sausage shape placed underneath the two rows of balls. These will be your petals.

Once you master the art of making these pretty delights, you will be decorating everything – even wedding cakes!

3 Fold the bottom half of the bag up to the top so that it covers all of the icing. Working on the outside of the bag, use your finger to push each ball firmly from the bottom to the top, making the edge at the top thinner than the bottom. When each ball has been squashed, run your finger gently halfway across the top of the petal. Use the same action to flatten the sausage.

4 Unpeel the half of the bag covering the icing to expose the petals, taking care that the petals stay in position.

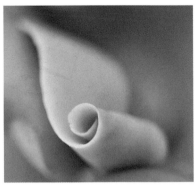

5 Lift the sausage shape off the plastic and curl into shape with the thinnest part at the top. This is the inner petal.

6 Place one of the petals on the side of the inner petal, thinnest part facing up. Fold the petal around the inner shape, closing the left side and leaving the right side open. Tuck the second petal into the open side of the first petal, closing the first petal around the back of the second petal.

7 Take the third petal, tuck it into the open side of the second petal and this time close the third petal on the right, making a second layer of the rose.

8 Repeat with the remaining five petals, so that your rose has three layers.

9 Shape the petals by gently holding the rose in your left hand and curl the petals delicately at the edges.

10 Gently squeeze the base of the rose by twisting around in your left hand and then snip the bottom excess tail with scissors.

To store

Lay the rose upwards on greaseproof paper or a chopping board to dry. (Do not refrigerate as the icing will absorb water and become soggy.) Repeat for the remaining pieces to make seven more roses. Store in a dry place at room temperature for approximately six months, but check the 'use by' date on the fondant icing pack.

Violet & rose creams

Traditionally a Victorian sweet, the subtle flavour of the rose or violet emerges as the chocolate coating melts in your mouth. These creams are irresistible and a true indulgence. They are unbelievably easy to make and are now top of my list of sweets to make as a gift. Beware – make lots, or you'll eat them before you've had time to wrap them up!

INGREDIENTS

MAKES 30 CREAMS

350 g (11½ oz) fondant icing

1 tbsp liquid glucose

1 tbsp violet syrup or rose water

Pink food colouring for rose creams, purple for violet creams (optional)

200 g (7 oz) good-quality plain chocolate, chopped

Cornflour

Small sugar flowers or piped flowers, to decorate

1 Mix together all the ingredients, except the chocolate and cornflour, in a food processor or by hand. The mixture should have a loose consistency but firm enough to handle. To make both violet and rose creams from one batch, divide the mixture into two and add half the quantity of flavouring and the colouring to the separate bowls.

2 Dust your hands very lightly with cornflour when handling the mixture. Form approximately 30 small ovals and leave to dry overnight on greaseproof baking paper or silicone.

3 Melt the chocolate in a bain-marie or put it in a small bowl set over a saucepan of gently simmering water. Don't let the bowl touch the water. Heat gently until the chocolate has melted. Remove from the heat and allow to cool slightly.

4 Dip the creams into the chocolate, then leave to dry on a cooling rack. When the chocolates have cooled slightly, add a sugar flower (attach with a dab of icing) or pipe a royal icing flower decoration on top. Allow the chocolates to set completely. Store in an airtight container in a cool, dry place for up to one month.

Pink coconut ice

This is a sweet that brings back all the charm of childhood and makes everyone wide-eyed at the memories of cooking as a child. A traditional English sweet that always sells well at fetes or bazaars, this no-cook recipe is easy and popular with all the family.

INGREDIENTS

397 g (14 oz) tin of condensed milk

340 g (12 oz) icing sugar

340 g (12 oz) desiccated coconut

Pink food colouring

1 Lightly grease and line a 20 cm (8 in) square or round tin with baking parchment.

2 Pour the condensed milk into a large mixing bowl and add the icing sugar. Beat well and mix in the desiccated coconut. The mixture will become firm and difficult to stir, but keep going until everything is well combined.

3 Divide the mixture into two separate bowls. Add a few drops of food colouring to one half of the mixture and mix in well.

4 Spread the remaining plain half evenly on the bottom of the tin and then spread the other colour on the top. Put in the fridge and leave to set overnight or until firm.

5 When set, use a sharp knife to cut into squares. Remove the squares from the tin and serve on a vintage tea plate or wrap in pretty muslin or fabric and give as a present.

Chocolate-coated toffee balls

These are such fun. They are hard, so roll them into very small balls so they are bite-sized and don't pull your teeth out! They make beautiful gifts if wrapped up in cellophane and tied with a ribbon or put into glass jars and decorated with ribbon.

1 Put all the toffee ingredients into a large saucepan and melt together over a medium heat, stirring continuously until all the sugar has dissolved. Bring to the boil and then simmer until the mixture reaches 116°C (240°F) on a sugar thermometer, the soft ball stage (see page 64), stirring occasionally.

2 Allow to cool to a comfortable temperature so that you can handle the mixture, but don't allow the mixture to cool so much that it starts to set. Roll pieces of the warm mixture with your fingers to make very small, bite-sized balls. Place the balls on a sheet of greaseproof paper and leave to cool completely.

3 Put the chocolate into a bain-marie or a bowl set over a saucepan of simmering water. Do not allow the bowl to touch the water. Heat gently until the chocolate is completely melted. Remove from the heat.

4 Dip the toffee balls one by one into the chocolate, then drop each ball into a small cup and sprinkle with hundreds and thousands. Swirl the ball around in the cup so that the hundreds and thousands coat it, then place the ball on a sheet of greaseproof paper to set. Store in an airtight container.

INGREDIENTS

FOR THE TOFFEE

250 ml (8 fl oz) double cream

300 g (9 oz) caster sugar

55 g (2 oz) cocoa powder

1 tbsp honey

25 g (1 oz) butter

FOR THE COATING

115 g (4 oz) good-quality plain chocolate, chopped

Hundreds and thousands

Hard candies

Hard candies are messy to make, but very satisfying as they look so impressive. It helps if you have a marble slab when moulding them, but you can use a greased worksurface. When pulling the candy to achieve the stripe, take care not to burn your fingers as time is of the essence when handling the hot sugar.

1 Mix the sugar and 150 ml (¼ pint) water together and place in a heavy-based saucepan. Bring to the boil, stirring continuously.

2 Add the liquid glucose and cream of tartar to the mixture. Boil over a medium heat until the temperature reaches 154°C (310°F) on a sugar thermometer, without stirring. Brush the sides of the pan with water using a pastry brush at regular intervals, to prevent sugar crystallization. When the right temperature is reached, remove the pan from the heat.

3 Pour one large pool (about 80 per cent of the mixture) and one small pool onto a marble slab or a greased work surface. Add a few drops of flavouring and food colouring to the smaller batch and mix with a wooden spoon.

4 When the mixtures are cool enough to handle, but haven't set too hard, take the larger pool of candy and pull it with your hands so that you are stretching it into a long ribbon. Pull the coloured candy so that it is the same length and then twist the two strands together to achieve a striped effect.

5 Either cut the candy with scissors into small pieces or pull, cut and shape into a heart. If you would like to finish with a sugar coating, roll the candy pieces in a bowl of granulated sugar before they have set. Cool on a silicone sheet or greaseproof paper until the candy has set. Stored in an airtight container, they should keep for several weeks.

INGREDIENTS

575 g (1¼ lb) granulated or caster sugar

180 g (6 oz) liquid glucose

½ tsp cream of tartar

Food colouring

Food flavouring

Granulated sugar, to coat (optional)

Chocolate Easter eggs

Making your own Easter eggs couldn't be easier with this simple recipe – just choose the mould of your choice and off you go. Chocolate eggs are simple to make and cost a lot less than shop-bought eggs and make original and perfect gifts.

INGREDIENTS

100 g (3¹/₂ oz) good-quality plain or white chocolate, chopped (the amount of chocolate will depend on the size of the mould)

Melted chocolate, royal icing, sugar flowers (see page 8) and ribbon, to decorate, optional

1 Melt the chocolate in a bain-marie or put it in a small bowl set over a saucepan of gently simmering water. Don't let the bowl touch the water. Heat gently until the chocolate has melted. Remove from the heat and allow to cool slightly.

2 Clean the Easter egg moulds thoroughly, polishing them with a cotton wool bud. This makes it easier to turn out the finished chocolate eggs.

3 Using a small paintbrush, coat the insides of the mould with a thin coating of chocolate. Put the moulds into the fridge for approximately 10 minutes.

Shop-bought sugar flowers or decorations brighten up the eggs, or make your own sugar flowers (see pages 8–11 for instructions).

If the melted chocolate starts to set in the bowl, return to the heat and warm through gently until smooth.

4 Repeat by painting another layer of chocolate, then return to the fridge for another 10 minutes. Repeat until you have three or four layers of chocolate. Leave the last layer in the mould for 20 minutes.

6 Place a non-stick baking tray in the oven until hot. Remove from the oven and put the edges of the eggs face down on the hot tray for 2–3 seconds only so they melt slightly. Stick the halves together. Place in the fridge for 5 minutes.

5 When the chocolate is completely set, gently remove the egg from the mould.

To decorate the eggs
Handle them as little as possible, or they will melt in your hands. Place the egg in a glass or on a secure surface so that it can't slide or move around. Using either royal icing or melted chocolate, pipe writing or a design onto the egg. Use home-made sugar roses (see page 8) or shop-bought sugar flowers to decorate further, using a small dot of melted chocolate to stick them in place.

Classic fudge

First invented in the 1880s, these creamy succulent squares are now a popular delight. Try livening up the basic recipe with cherries, nuts, vanilla or chocolate.

1 Lightly grease and line a 20 cm (8 in) square tin with baking parchment.

2 Put all the ingredients into a large non-stick saucepan. Heat gently, stirring with a wooden spoon until all the sugar has dissolved. Bring to the boil and simmer gently for 10–15 minutes, stirring continuously until the temperature reaches 116°C (240°F) on a sugar thermometer or test using the 'soft ball' method – drop a little of the mixture into a jug of cold water. If it forms a soft ball, the fudge is ready.

3 Remove the pan from the heat. Beat the mixture with a wooden spoon for 5–10 minutes, until it is thick and grainy and the shine is taken off. Pour into the tin and use a sharp knife to score the surface into squares, taking care not to cut all the way through.

4 When cool, cut into squares and remove from the tin. Fudge can be stored in an airtight container for up to 1 month.

For a different flavour, try adding the following ingredients at the beating stage:

FRUIT & NUT: Add *40 g (1½ oz) each of glacé cherries and pecans, chopped.*

RUM & RAISIN: *Stir in 2 tbsp of dark rum mixed with 115 g (4 oz) of chopped raisins.*

VANILLA: *Substitute the demerara sugar for caster sugar and add 1 tsp vanilla extract or 1 vanilla pod.*

CHOCOLATE: *Stir in 175 g (6 oz) of good-quality melted plain chocolate.*

Caramel bites

These delicious bites have just the right mix of a crunchy base, succulent caramel and chocolate topping that just melts in your mouth. Make plenty – they will disappear very quickly!

1 Preheat the oven to 180°C/350°F/Gas 4. Line a 23 x 33 cm (9 x 13 in) Swiss roll tin with lightly greased baking parchment.

2 To make the shortbread, blend all the ingredients in a food processor or mix with a wooden spoon. When the dough is well mixed, bring together using your hands and press into the lined tin. Prick the shortbread base with a fork and bake for about 15 minutes.

3 To make the caramel, put all the ingredients in a saucepan and heat slowly until the butter is fully melted. Bring to the boil, stirring continuously for 8–10 minutes.

4 Test to see if the mixture has reached the soft ball stage (drop a small amount of mixture into a glass of cold water – if it forms a ball, the mixture is ready) or 116°C (240°F) on a sugar thermometer. Cook for a few minutes and then remove from the heat. Pour the caramel over the shortbread and spread evenly. Leave to set.

5 When the caramel is completely set, melt the milk chocolate in a bain-marie or put it in a small bowl set over a saucepan of gently simmering water. Don't let the bowl touch the water. Heat gently until the chocolate has melted. Spread the chocolate over the caramel.

6 To decorate, either grate white chocolate over the top or score with a fork when the chocolate has cooled slightly. When the chocolate has set, cut into small bite-sized squares. These are best eaten straight away, but will keep for a few days stored in a biscuit tin.

INGREDIENTS

FOR THE SHORTBREAD
55 g (2 oz) cornflour
225 g (8 oz) plain flour
55 g (2 oz) icing sugar
225 g (8 oz) unsalted butter

FOR THE CARAMEL
115 g (4 oz) butter
115 g (4 oz) sugar
2 tbsp golden syrup
175 g (6 oz) tin of condensed milk

TO DECORATE
115 g (4 oz) milk chocolate
Grated white chocolate (optional)

Apple jellies

Jelly sweets are real comfort food and delicious made using any fruit that has a thick pulp – also try pears, apricots or plums. A selection of colours will look like jewels in a gift box.

1 Roughly chop the apples, put in a pan and cover with just enough water to stop the fruit sticking during cooking. Bring to the boil, then simmer gently until the fruit is very soft. Sieve the pulp to remove any excess liquid or purée in a blender.

2 Weigh the fruit purée and return it to the pan with an equal amount of caster sugar. Put the pan back on the heat and stir in the lemon juice. Heat gently until the sugar has dissolved then boil rapidly until the mixture becomes a thick paste. Take the pan off the heat.

3 Dissolve the gelatine in a small amount of warm water following the pack instructions and add to the fruit paste, stirring thoroughly to mix. Pour the mixture onto a baking tray large enough to accommodate all the sweets and leave to set overnight.

4 Put the granulated sugar in a bowl. Using a small heart-shaped cutter, cut out the jellies and then roll each one in the granulated sugar until evenly coated. Lay the jellies on a sheet of greaseproof paper to dry at room temperature. Store in an airtight container, but do not refrigerate.

INGREDIENTS

1 kg (2 lb) apples, peeled and cored

Caster sugar

Freshly squeezed juice of 1 lemon

2 sachets of gelatine

125 g (4 oz) granulated sugar, to dust

Candied orange peel

These are the most delicate of gifts and my favourite treat of all time. They are lovely to make and the aroma of the cooking oranges makes this a perfect winter activity. These make great Christmas presents.

1 Score the oranges into quarters using either a sharp knife or a citrus scorer. Peel the oranges carefully, trying to keep the peels intact. Set the oranges aside and use in a separate recipe. Using a sharp knife, cut away as much of the white pith from the peels as possible – don't worry if some remains. Slice the peel lengthways into strips approximately 1 cm (½ in) wide.

2 Put the sugar and water in a saucepan over a medium heat and boil for 5 minutes. Add the strips of peel and reduce the heat to a slow simmer on the lowest setting. Do not stir. Simmer gently for 2 hours until the syrup reduces to approximately one quarter of its original

INGREDIENTS

4 large oranges

1 litre (1³/4 pints) water

275 g (9 oz) caster sugar,
plus extra for coating

300 g (10 oz) good-quality
plain chocolate

volume. Remove the saucepan from the heat and allow the mixture to cool. Once cooled, drain the peels.

3 Preheat the oven to a very low temperature, approximately 85°C/ 200°F/Gas ¼. Put the caster sugar in a bowl and dip the peels in the sugar, coating them evenly. Place them on a baking sheet lined with baking parchment and sprinkle with more sugar if necessary.

4 Place the peels in the cool oven for 1 hour to allow them to dry out. Check at 20-minute intervals to ensure that the peels aren't cooking. Alternatively, leave on a drying rack overnight. Once the peels are completely dry, scrape off any excess sugar clumps.

5 Put the chocolate in a bain-marie or a small bowl set over a saucepan of gently simmering water. Don't let the bowl touch the water. Heat gently until the chocolate has melted. Dip each piece of peel into the chocolate at least halfway. Leave the chocolate-coated peel strips to set on a drying rack. Store in an airtight container.

Tie the strips of peel into small bundles and serve as a treat with after-dinner coffee.

Almond nut brittle with orange zest

These traditional crunchy bites have the magical ingredient of a hint of orange and will be a hit with family and friends of any age; they are also quick and easy and are an instant crowd pleaser. The almonds have to be baked first in the oven – take care not to forget about them or the mixture will taste burnt.

1 Preheat the oven to 180°C/350°F/Gas 4.

2 Spread the whole almonds in a 23 cm (9 in) square baking tin, lined with baking parchment. Gently roast in the oven for approximately 10 minutes or until they are light golden. Set aside.

3 Put the sugar and golden syrup in a heavy-based saucepan and heat over a low heat until all the sugar has dissolved and reaches the soft-crack stage, 132°C (270°F) on a sugar thermometer, stirring continuously. Remove from the heat and stir in the flaked almonds and orange zest.

4 Pour the sugar syrup into the baking tin and flatten slightly with a metal spoon. Leave to cool.

5 When the brittle is completely solid, turn it out onto a work surface or chopping board and break it up into shards using a small hammer or rolling pin. Store in an airtight container.

INGREDIENTS

200 g (7 oz) whole almonds, blanched

450 g (14 oz) granulated sugar

2 tbsp golden syrup

100 g (3 1/2 oz) flaked almonds

Finely grated zest of 1 orange

Chocolate drops

Chocolate drops are very easy to create and great to make with children. You can play around with the decoration – try using hundreds and thousands, sugared flowers, crystallized fruit or nuts to create your own unique style.

1 Line a baking sheet with greaseproof paper or baking parchment.

2 Put the chocolate in a bain-marie or in a small bowl set over a saucepan of gently simmering water. Don't let the bowl touch the water. Heat gently until the chocolate has melted.

3 Fill a piping bag with the melted chocolate, or use a teaspoon, and pour drops of chocolate onto the prepared baking sheet. Use the back of a metal spoon to shape the chocolate into circular, bite-sized discs about 3 cm (1½ in) in diameter.

4 To decorate, melt some contrasting chocolate in a bain-marie or a bowl (as above) and drizzle thin lines of chocolate over the chocolate drops. Use cocktail sticks to create shapes with the drizzled chocolate.

5 Alternatively, you could simply grate the chocolate over the drops or sprinkle chopped almonds or hundreds and thousands over them before they set. Store in the fridge in an airtight container or a cardboard box.

INGREDIENTS

100 g (3½ oz) white or good-quality plain chocolate, chopped

White, plain and milk chocolate, to decorate

Choice of toppings (see step 5)

As well as these elegant versions, encourage children to create their own decorations.

Mini gingerbread men

These are so cute! You can buy all sorts of shapes and sizes of gingerbread men cutters in the shops. Here I have used a small cutter as it makes more biscuits to go around! These also look great hung on the Christmas tree.

1 Preheat the oven to 190°C/375°F/Gas 5. Lightly grease three large baking trays with either vegetable oil or butter.

2 Put the flour, bicarbonate of soda and ginger into a bowl. Rub in the butter until the mixture resembles breadcrumbs. Stir in the sugar and then add the golden syrup and egg to the mixture. Mix to form a dough, kneading lightly with your hands if necessary.

3 Lightly flour your work surface and divide the dough in half. Roll out one half to a thickness of 5 mm (¼ in). Using a gingerbread man cutter, cut out the shapes and place them onto the baking trays. Decorate by using currants for eyes and buttons. Repeat using the other half of the dough mixture.

4 Bake in the oven for 10–12 minutes until a dark golden colour. Leave the gingerbread men to cool slightly before transferring to a cooling rack. Leave to cool completely. Tie ribbon bows around the gingerbread men to decorate. Store in an airtight container or a biscuit tin and eat within a week.

INGREDIENTS

350 g (12 oz) plain flour

1 tsp bicarbonate of soda

1 tsp ground ginger

115 g (4 oz) unsalted butter

175 g (6 oz) light muscovado sugar

4 tbsp golden syrup

1 free-range egg, beaten

Currants and ribbon, to decorate

Honeycomb

This all-time favourite was traditionally given as a love token. There will probably be no need to store it – it's so popular, it'll all be eaten in a day. You can also try serving it sprinkled on vanilla ice cream for a delicious dessert.

1 Line a shallow 23 cm (9 in) square baking tray with baking parchment.

2 Put the honey, syrup, sugar and 5 tablespoons of water in a large heavy-based saucepan and heat gently over a medium heat, stirring occasionally until the sugar dissolves.

3 Increase the heat and cook until the mixture reaches 149°C (300°F) on a sugar thermometer. Take off the heat and add the bicarbonate of soda. The mixture will fizz up into a foam. Immediately pour into the prepared baking tray.

4 Leave to cool for approximately 1 hour, then break up and serve. Store in an airtight container.

INGREDIENTS

75 g (2¹/₂ oz) clear honey

140 g (4¹/₂ oz) golden syrup

400 g (13 oz) caster sugar

2 tsp bicarbonate of soda

Lemon goodie gumdrops

These little treats are fun and easy to make and a great project to do with children. The consistency is squidgey and sticky and a far healthier treat without all the additives in shop-bought gums. Make them with either lemon juice or any other flavouring you have to hand.

1 Grease a 23 cm (9 in) square baking tray with a good amount of butter and set aside.

2 Mix the sugar and 125 ml (4 fl oz) cold water in a medium saucepan and bring to the boil over a medium heat. Stir continuously. To prevent sugar crystallization, brush the sides of the pan with a pastry brush dipped in cold water several times during the process.

3 Dissolve the gelatine in the hot water, making sure that all the gelatine crystals have dissolved and then add the gelatine to the mixture in the saucepan and boil for 15 minutes, stirring continuously.

4 Add the lemon juice and zest to the mixture and boil for a further 5 minutes. Add a few drops of food colouring.

5 Pour the mixture into the baking tray and put aside to set for approximately 3 hours.

6 Butter a sharp knife and a pair of scissors and cut the set sweets into small pieces. Alternatively, use a small round cutter to make bite-sized circles. Put the caster sugar in a bowl and roll the pieces in the sugar to coat them evenly. Store in an airtight container for several weeks.

INGREDIENTS

400 g (13 oz) granulated sugar

4 sachets of gelatine

125 ml (4 fl oz) hot (not boiling) water, for dissolving gelatine

Freshly-squeezed juice of 1 lemon

Grated zest of 1 unwaxed lemon or 1 orange

Yellow food colouring

Approximately 100 g (3½ oz) caster sugar, to coat

Jewel-coloured lollipops

You can buy all sorts of shapes and sizes of moulds for lollipops and these are a great project to do with children. They are so quick and easy and you don't have to make them with moulds. When the sugar cools slightly, it becomes easy to mould into any shape. A fantastic treat!

1 Wash, dry and butter the lollipop moulds. If you don't have moulds you can use a silicone sheet or buttered greaseproof paper.

2 Mix the sugar, liquid glucose and 4 tablespoons of water in a saucepan. Cook over a medium heat, stirring with a wooden spoon until the mixture comes to the boil. To prevent sugar crystallization, use a pastry brush dipped in cold water and brush down the sides of the pan at regular intervals.

3 Boil the mixture without stirring until it reaches 149°C (300°F) on a sugar thermometer. Remove from the heat. Mix in a few drops of food colouring and any flavouring. I used 1 tablespoon of lemon juice for the yellow lollies, 1 tablespoon of orange blossom water for the orange lollies and 1 tablespoon of strawberry flavouring for the red lollies.

4 Put the lolly sticks into the moulds and then carefully pour the mixture into each mould, ensuring that it doesn't spill over the top. If you don't have moulds, use a teaspoon to gently spoon and shape a lolly on a silicone sheet or greaseproof paper. Set aside and leave to cool at room temperature.

5 If storing, wrap the lollies individually in cellophane or greaseproof paper and place in an airtight container.

INGREDIENTS

Butter, for greasing

200 g (7 oz) granulated sugar

85 g (3 oz) liquid glucose

Food colouring

Food flavouring, such as lemon juice, orange blossom water, strawberry flavouring, peppermint flavouring or rose water

These lollies make a great treat for Valentine's Day.

Marshmallows

Cut your home-made marshmallows into big chunks to eat as a sweet, or cut into smaller chunks and serve with a big mug of hot chocolate. They also look fantastic served on a party table.

1 Sift together the icing sugar and cornflour in a bowl. Grease a 20 cm (8 in) square shallow cake tin with a little vegetable oil, then shake the icing sugar and cornflour mixture to coat the tin. Set aside.

2 Pour the hot water into a bowl, sprinkle the gelatine on top and stir gently until the gelatine crystals dissolve. Add 2–3 drops of food colouring to the gelatine and mix thoroughly. (Pink is traditionally used, but you can use whichever colour you wish.)

3 Put the egg whites into a food processor and set aside. Put the granulated sugar into a medium saucepan and add 250 ml (8 fl oz) of water. Stir over a low heat until the sugar has completely dissolved. Increase the heat and bring the mixture to a boil. In the meantime, turn on the food processor and mix the egg whites until they form stiff peaks. Boil the sugar mixture until it reaches 121°C (250°F), the hard ball stage – when a small amount of mixture is dropped into water it will form a ball that holds its shape. Take the pan off the heat.

4 Pour the gelatine into the pan of syrup, stirring continuously until the gelatine is thoroughly mixed with the syrup. Turn the food processor back on and carefully pour the syrup onto the beating egg whites. Continue mixing until the mixture turns thick and bulky but is still pourable. If you lift up the beater, a ribbon of marshmallow should remain on the surface for a few seconds before sinking back down into the mix.

INGREDIENTS

1 tbsp icing sugar

1 tbsp cornflour

125 ml (4 fl oz) hot water

25 g (1 oz) sachet gelatine

Red food colouring

2 free-range egg whites

500 g (1 lb) granulated sugar

5 Pour the marshmallow into the prepared tin and leave to set in a cool place for approximately 1 or 2 hours (do not refrigerate).

6 Dust a chopping board or work surface with the remaining cornflour and icing sugar mixture. Butter a sharp knife and carefully ease the marshmallow mixture out of the tin and onto the board. Sift any extra icing sugar and cornflour over the marshmallow if necessary. Cut the marshmallow into cubes.

7 Store in an airtight tin lined with baking parchment or greaseproof paper for up to one week. You can freeze marshmallows – they will only take a minute or two to defrost.

Mini florentines

A complete favourite with everyone. Who can resist the chocolate as it melts it your mouth, followed by the crispness of the nuts and the chewiness of the fruits? This recipe uses dark chocolate, but also try making with either milk chocolate or white chocolate or a mixture of both. These make very impressive treats when presented in a small box or wrapped in cellophane and tied with pretty ribbon.

INGREDIENTS

55 g (2 oz) unsalted butter

55 g (2 oz) demerara sugar

55 g (2 oz) golden syrup

55 g (2 oz) plain flour

4 glacé cherries, finely chopped

55 g (2 oz) mixed candied peel, finely chopped

55 g (2 oz) mixed almonds and walnuts, finely chopped

175 g (6 oz) good-quality plain chocolate, chopped

1 Preheat the oven to 180°C/350°F/Gas 4. Line three baking trays with non-stick baking paper.

2 Put the butter, sugar and syrup into a saucepan and heat gently until the butter has melted. Remove from the heat. Add the flour, cherries, candied peel and nuts to the mixture and stir well. Spoon half teaspoonfuls of the mixture onto the baking trays, allowing space to expand as they cook.

3 Bake in the oven for 8–10 minutes or until golden brown. Allow to cool on the paper before transferring them to a cooling rack. Leave to cool completely.

4 Put the chocolate in a bain-marie or in a bowl set over a saucepan of gently simmering water. Do not let the bowl touch the water. Heat gently until the chocolate is completely melted.

5 Spread a small amount of melted chocolate over the base of each florentine. Leave to set, chocolate side up, on the cooling rack. Store in an airtight container for up to one week.

Peppermint creams

These are great to make with small children who are starting to take an interest in cooking. They also make a sophisticated gift dipped in rich dark chocolate or served as after-dinner mints.

INGREDIENTS

225 g (8 oz) icing sugar

1 free-range egg white

Peppermint essence

Food colouring (optional)

1 Lightly grease a large piece of greaseproof paper. Sift approximately two-thirds of the icing sugar into a mixing bowl. Lightly whisk the egg white with a fork until it is lightly frothy. Pour the beaten egg white into the icing sugar, add a few drops of peppermint essence and mix with a fork until all the ingredients are combined.

2 Add the remaining icing sugar a little at a time and continue mixing until the dough is too stiff to mix with a fork. Finish mixing with your hands until the mixture has a doughy consistency. Taste and add more peppermint if necessary. Keep your hands dusted with icing sugar so that the mixture doesn't stick to your fingers. Add a few drops of food colouring if required.

3 Dust your work surface with icing sugar and roll out the dough to a thickness of 1 cm (½ in). With a small round cutter, cut out the peppermint creams and lay on the sheet of greaseproof paper to dry.

For chocolate-dipped peppermint creams

Chop 200 g (7 oz) of good-quality plain chocolate and put in a bain-marie or a bowl set over a saucepan of gently simmering water (do not let the bowl touch the water). Heat gently, stirring occasionally until all the chocolate has melted. Remove from the heat. Carefully dip the peppermint creams (one at a time) halfway into the chocolate and gently place them on a cooling rack or greaseproof paper to dry, then put them in the fridge to set. If the chocolate starts to set when you're in the middle of dipping the creams, place the bowl back on the pan of hot water, heat and stir very gently until the chocolate melts again.

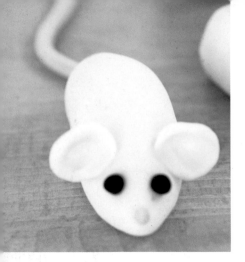

Sugar mice

Don't be put off by the moulding as there are very few parts and it takes very little skill to make these sweet mice.

INGREDIENTS

500 g (1 lb) pack white fondant icing

Small amount of black fondant icing (for eyes)

Food colouring (pink or yellow for body)

Cornflour

1 For a coloured mouse, break off a piece of white fondant icing and add a few drops of food colouring.

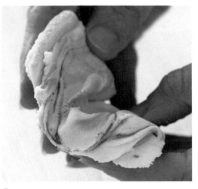

2 Spread the colouring evenly through the fondant by kneading it gently.

3 Dust your work surface with a little cornflour. Knead the icing so that it's soft to handle and any colouring is evenly blended.

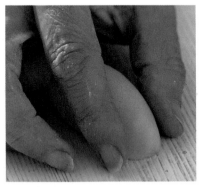

4 Mould a piece of icing into shape for the body.

These cute mice make a wonderful gift
to tuck into Christmas stockings.

You can buy fondant icing in 500 g (1 lb) packs, but you need very little to make these mice.

5 Next, make the ears. Make a small sausage shape and cut it in half. Roll each piece into a circle and indent the centre with the back of a paintbrush or a sugarpaste moulding tool.

6 Attach the ears in place on the body, using a dab of water to stick them down.

7 For the eyes, make a small sausage shape from black icing and cut it in half. Roll each piece into a small ball and attach it to the face using a dab of water.

8 Next, make the nose from a small ball and attach it in place with a dab of water.

9 Finally, make a long thin sausage for the tail and attach it in place as before.

10 Leave the mouse to dry. Store in a cardboard box at room temperature – do not refrigerate. Sugarpaste can keep for a long time, but is best eaten within 6 months.

Toffee apples

What is Bonfire Night without a toffee apple? If possible, make these in the apple season and use freshly picked apples or bought from a farmer's market, as the toffee sticks better to these than the shop-bought ones.

1 Wash and dry the apples thoroughly. Push a wooden skewer or lolly stick into the core of each apple nearly the whole way down, but not so that they poke through the other end. Prepare a baking tray (large enough to hold 4 apples) with greaseproof paper.

2 Put the sugar, butter and ½ tablespoon of water in a saucepan and heat gently, stirring occasionally. Increase the heat and boil until you reach 132°C (270°F) on a sugar thermometer (soft-crack stage), without stirring.

3 Take the saucepan off the heat and dip the apples into the toffee mixture one at a time, coating the apples evenly all over. Stand the apples on the prepared baking tray and leave to set. These are best eaten immediately.

INGREDIENTS
4 crisp eating apples
115 g (4 oz) caster sugar
25 g (1 oz) unsalted butter

Chocolate truffles

Truffles look and taste very luxurious – and they are a joy to make. Here is a basic recipe where I have added either brandy or orange juice, but have fun at trying out different flavours.

1 In a bowl, soften the butter and then add the icing sugar, beating slowly until the mixture is fluffy.

2 Put the chocolate into a bain-marie or a bowl set over a saucepan of gently simmering water. Do not allow the bowl to touch the water. Heat gently until the chocolate is completely melted and smooth. Remove from the heat and allow to cool for a few minutes.

3 Stir the melted chocolate into the butter icing mix and add the brandy or orange juice and zest, if using. Refrigerate until firm.

4 Roll small pieces of the truffle mix into bite-sized balls and then roll in cocoa powder, grated chocolate or chopped nuts. Store in the fridge in an airtight container for up to a month.

INGREDIENTS

115 g (4 oz) unsalted butter

115 g (4 oz) icing sugar

115 g (4 oz) good-quality plain chocolate, chopped

2 tsp brandy or freshly squeezed juice and zest of 1 orange (optional)

Chopped nuts, grated white or milk chocolate or cocoa powder, to coat

A box of truffles with different flavours makes the perfect gift for a chocoholic!

Turkish delight

An exotic treat traditionally from the Middle East, this is said to date back over 200 years and originally served as a love token. This is a fun and sticky project to make with children.

1 Lightly grease a shallow 20 cm (8 in) square cake tin with a small amount of vegetable oil. Mix the sugar, 125 ml (4 fl oz) water, lemon and orange juice together in a saucepan. Heat over a medium heat, stirring until the sugar has completely dissolved. Increase the heat and boil without stirring until the mixture reaches 116°C (240°F) on a sugar thermometer (soft ball stage). Take the saucepan off the heat. Gently stir in the cream of tartar. Leave to cool for 10–15 minutes.

2 Mix 100 ml (3½ fl oz) of cold water in a measuring jug with the cornflour. Add the measured hot water into the cornflour mixture and stir. Pour the cornflour liquid into a separate saucepan. Bring to the boil slowly over a low heat stirring continuously until the mixture is thick and smooth. Take off the heat.

3 Carefully pour the hot sugar syrup a little at a time into the cornflour mixture, stirring with a wooden spoon. Put the saucepan back on the heat and slowly bring to a simmer. Cook gently for 25 minutes stirring occasionally to prevent sticking. Take off the heat.

4 Stir in the honey, rose water and a few drops of food colouring. Leave to cool for a couple of minutes and pour into the prepared tin. Set aside and leave to cool completely then put in the fridge to set overnight.

5 Sift some icing sugar over your work surface. Run a knife around the edge of the tin and invert the tin onto the work surface. Sift more icing sugar over the Turkish Delight and cut into squares. Store in an airtight tin in a cool place. Fresh Turkish delight is best eaten within a few days.

INGREDIENTS
500 g (1 lb) granulated sugar

Juice of ½ a lemon

Juice of ½ an orange

¼ tsp cream of tartar

75 g (3 oz) cornflour

500 ml (17 fl oz) hot water

2 tbsp clear honey

1 tsp rose water

Pink food colouring

Icing sugar

Christmas cookie decorations

These festive cookies look particularly impressive hung on a Christmas tree or in front of candles or a window so the light shines through the candy centres.

1 Mix all the dough ingredients in a food processor until the mixture forms a ball, or mix together by hand in a large bowl. If the mixture is too wet add a little flour, if it is too dry add a few drops of water. Wrap the dough in a plastic bag and leave to rest in the fridge for about an hour.

2 Preheat the oven to 180°C/350°F/Gas 4. Roll the dough out on a sheet of greaseproof paper to a depth of approximately 1 cm (½ in). Using Christmas cutters, cut out your desired shapes from the dough, then cut out a hole in the centre for the sweet window. Using a small cutter or the tip of a large round piping nozzle, make a small hole at the top, large enough to insert a hanging loop of ribbon or thread.

3 Place the cookies on a large baking tray lined with baking parchment and bake in the oven for 10 minutes or until the cookies have turned a golden colour.

4 Meanwhile, use a rolling pin to crush the hard sweets in their paper or in a plastic bag. When the cookies are ready, remove from the oven and fill up the space in the centre of each cookie with an even layer of crushed sweets. Don't go over the edges of the biscuit. Bake for a further 2 minutes, but don't allow the sweets to bubble or caramelize or they will lose their colour.

5 Leave to cool. Store in an airtight container at room temperature. When ready to hang, thread ribbon through the hole and tie a knot.

INGREDIENTS

FOR THE COOKIES

2 free-range eggs

115 g (4 oz) caster sugar

115 g (4 oz) soft brown sugar

150 ml (5 fl oz) golden syrup

175 g (6 oz) butter

1 tsp ground ginger

½ tsp ground cinnamon

½ tsp bicarbonate of soda

750 g (1½ lb) plain flour

FOR THE FILLING

Hard-boiled sweets in a variety of colours

White and red fondant icing rolled into tiny balls, to decorate

Zesty almond crunchies

The real twist in these bites is the zest of the orange. The citrus aroma wakes up your sense of smell as the crunchiness of the almonds kick in, then the chocolate melts in the mouth making a brilliant combination of textures and flavour.

1 Line a large baking sheet with baking parchment.

2 Put the chocolate and butter into a bain-marie or in a bowl set over a saucepan of gently simmering water. Do not allow the bowl to touch the water. Heat gently until the chocolate and butter are completely melted and smooth. Remove from the heat.

3 Mix in the flaked almonds and the orange zest. Spoon small portions onto the lined baking tray and leave to cool in the fridge. Store in an airtight container in the fridge.

INGREDIENTS

MAKES APPROX 20 SPLINTERS

225 g (8 oz) good-quality plain chocolate

15 g (1/2 oz) unsalted butter

150 g (5 oz) flaked almonds

Grated zest of 1 medium orange

Sugar temperatures for sweet-making

If these recipes have inspired you to make lots of sweets, it would be well worthwhile buying a sugar thermometer as this is the most accurate way to measure the temperature of sugar.

Thread stage	106–112°C (223–234°F)	Fruit pastes	When drizzled, a spoonful of sugar forms a thin, fine thread.
Soft-ball stage	112–116°C (234–240°F)	Creams, fondant, fudge	When dropped into very cold water, a small quantity of sugar forms a ball, but does not retain its shape when pressed with fingers.
Firm-ball stage	118–120°C (244–248°F)	Caramel	When dropped into very cold water, a small quantity of sugar forms a ball which holds its shape but is sticky when pressed.
Hard-ball stage	121–130°C (250–266°F)	Marshmallow	When dropped into very cold water, a small quantity of sugar forms a ball which holds its shape yet is still pliable.
Soft-crack stage	231–143°C (270–290°F)	Butterscotch, toffee	When dropped into very cold water, a small quantity of sugar can be stretched between your fingers, separating out into hard strands.
Hard-crack stage	149–154°C (300–310°F)	Nut brittle	When dropped into very cold water, a small quantity of sugar will solidify, separating into brittle threads.
Light caramel stage	160–170°C (320–335°F)	Glazes	When poured onto a white saucer, the sugar syrup will have a golden colour.
Dark caramel stage	177°C (up to 350°F)	Glazes	When poured onto a white saucer, the sugar syrup will have a dark amber colour.

The secret to sweet success is temperature. The temperature of cooked sugar determines whether it becomes a caramel, a toffee or a hard sweet. You must have patience. Sometimes the temperature gauge will look as though it's never going to move and then all of a sudden it will shoot up. Keep an eye on it at all times and as soon as it reaches the exact temperature, take the pan straight off the heat.